Ever since the publication of the original LETTERS FROM CAMP more than 15 years ago, I have been asked by parents, campers, and friends to compile a book of my all time favorite LETTERS FROM CAMP.

So here they are! After more than 1 million copies and many editions—the very best, the warmest, the funniest, the classic LETTERS FROM CAMP.

Bill Adler,

New York City

Bill Adler's All Time Great Classic Letters from Camp

Edited by Bill Adler, creator and editor of the original LETTERS FROM CAMP series

tempo books

GROSSET & DUNLAP
A FILMWAYS COMPANY
Publishers • New York

*BILL ADLER'S ALL TIME GREAT CLASSIC
LETTERS FROM CAMP*
Copyright © 1978 by Bill Adler Books, Inc.
All Rights Reserved
ISBN: 0-448-14748-3
A Tempo Books Original
Tempo Books is registered in the U.S. Patent Office
Published simultaneously in Canada
Printed in the United States of America

**Dedicated to the thousands of
parents, grandparents, aunts, and uncles
who have let me share these
letters from camp.**

Bill Adler's All Time Great Classic Letters from Camp

Dear Folks,
 Yesterday we went on a treasure hunt to look for a lost treasure. It was the gold watch Grandma gave me for graduation.

> Your son,
> Michael

Dear Folks:
 Camp is better than school, but that isn't saying much.

> Love,
> Roger

Dear Mom and Dad:
 We have air conditioning in the bunk now. One of the kids knocked out the window pane.

> Your son

Dear Parents:
 I love you and I miss you, but not too much.

> Stephanie

Dear Parents:
  Guess what I learned at camp?
Mosquitos like to eat kids.

> Denise

Dear Mom and Dad:
  It was very hot at camp today and we went swimming all day.
  It was a lot of fun and I found three water snakes and four turtles and a dead crocodile.

> Love,
> Amy

Dear Folks:
   There are 80 kids at camp and 4,200 bees and 2,100 mosquitos.

>   Your son,
>   Bill

Dear Folks:
   Our pet bird died.
   The funeral was yesterday.

>   Love,
>   Carole

Dear Mom and Dad:
   I think there are some spies at the camp.
   Somebody told the counselor I didn't take a bath.

>   Jack

Dear Folks:
    They get you up every morning at camp at 7 a.m.
    Next summer I want to go to a camp where they let you sleep until noon.

                        Your daughter

Dear Parents:
    This is the last letter I am writing this summer. I've got to have time for some fun.

                        Love,
                        Gwen

Dear Grandma and Grandpa:
　I brush my teeth twice a day.
　That is the most fun I have at camp.

　　　　　　　　　　Your granddaughter

Dear Freddy:
　I met a nice girl at camp.
　I think I love her because she wears eyeglasses like me.

　　　　　　　　　　Your friend,
　　　　　　　　　　Robbie

Dear Folks:
　Please send me a list of clothes that I brought to camp.
　So far I think I lost everything except two pair of underwear.

　　　　　　　　　　Mickey

Dear Mother and Father:
 Everybody runs to the mess hall because if you don't get to the food before the counselor, there isn't anything left.

>Your son,
>Gerold

Dear Stephanie:
 Remember the boy at camp that I wrote you about that I was in love with.
 Well I am not in love with him anymore.

>Your friend,
>Andrea

P.S. I will write you about the new boy I am in love with tomorrow.

Dear Mom and Dad:
    Poor kids are lucky.
    They don't have to go to camp.

                            Jennifer

Dear Mom and Dad:
    A bee stung me.
    I had to stand up all day.

                            Love,
                            Barbara

Dear Folks:
    The camp doctor is very nice.
    He doesn't make you take aspirin even if you are sick.

                            Harold

Dear Aunt Ellen:
   My parents gave me a camera so I could take a picture at camp and send it to all my relatives.
   What kind of picture do you want?
   The wallet size are 35 cents.

                                    Your nephew,
                                    Aaron

Dear Uncle Henry:
   I made you a surprise in arts and crafts.

                                    Love,
                                    Debbie
   P.S. What size belt do you wear?

Dear Grandma:
    I am starving at camp.
    Please send me candy before it is too late.

                      Love,
                      Your granddaughter

Dear Folks:
    I lost my left sneaker.
    Please send me another left sneaker as soon as possible because it isn't easy to run on one foot.

                      Your son,
                      David

Dear Mom and Dad:
    Monday was a holiday at camp.
    They gave us a hot meal.

                      Your son,
                      Phil

Dear Parents:
 They made me the cheerleader for the baseball team.
 When I grow up I am going to be the cheerleader for the New York Mets.

>   Love,
>   Your daughter

Dear Mom and Dad:
 We have a new counselor.
 His name is Rat Fink.
 The other counselor went home.
 His name was The Skunk.

>   Your son,
>   Andy

Dear Folks:
    Last night we slept in the woods.
    It was a lot of fun and I didn't sleep all night.

                              Love,
                              Betsy

Dear Parents:
    How are you?
    Please send me a big box of aspirin.

                              Jamie

Dear Folks:
    This is my best summer.
    I got the best sunburn in the whole camp.

                              Naomi

Dear Father:
 I hate my counselor.
 I hate the kids.
 I hate the food.
 I hate the weather.
 I hope I can come back here again next summer.

>   Your son,
>   Jay

Dear Mother and Father:
 Thank you for sending me to camp.
 It is very interesting.

>   Your son

P.S. The police left last night.

Dear Mom and Dad:
　　We have a nice bunk at camp and I have the best bed in the bunk because I am not under the hole in the roof.

　　　　　　　　　　　　Love,
　　　　　　　　　　　　Beatrice

Dear Folks:
　　I miss my brother at camp, but not much.

　　　　　　　　　　　　Love,
　　　　　　　　　　　　Claudine

Dear Folks:
　　Please send my doll to camp.
　　I need a friend.

　　　　　　　　　　　　Stephanie

Dear Mother and Father,
 I am taking good care of all my camp clothes. I find the best way to take care of them is to wear the same shirt and shorts so the others won't get ruined.

Love,
Michelle

Dear Mom and Dad:
    I have the best job at camp.
    I get to make the counselor's bed every day.

                        Love,
                        Vernon

Dear Parents:
    They don't have enough beds at camp.
    Last night I had to sleep with the dog.

                        Your son

Dear Mom and Dad:
    There are lots of things to do at camp if you don't like to have fun.

                        Sandy

Dear Mom and Dad:
I think you picked a good camp when you picked this camp for me.
This camp has everything.
Mosquitos, bugs, poison ivy, water snakes, and hurricanes.

       Love,
       Your son

Dear Parents:
I am fine.
They take good care of me at camp, but why do I have to brush my teeth every day if I haven't eaten in three days?

       Love,
       Naomi

Dear Larry:
    I am the richest kid in the whole camp.
    I am the only one with 25 Tom Seaver baseball trading cards.

                                    Your pal,
                                    Anthony

Dear Mom:
    How are you?
    I am fine except when I throw up.

                                    Love,
                                    Debbie

Dear Laura:
    There are 62 boys at this camp and I like them all except one.

                                    Your friend,
                                    Betty

Dear Aunt Susan and Uncle Bill:
 They gave a prize for the best eater at camp and I placed last.
 But I didn't care because I am a baseball player, not an eater.

                         Love,
                         Your nephew

Dear Mom:
 Please come up to camp and cook for me right away.
 I have been here 34 days and so far I have had two good meals and they were peanut butter and jelly sandwiches.

                         Love,
                         Beth

Dear Aunt Ruth:
　　This camp is terrific if you don't know any better.

　　　　　　　　　　　　Your nephew,
　　　　　　　　　　　　Lloyd

Dear Monty:
　　All the girls are dogs at this camp, even the one I am going to marry someday.

　　　　　　　　　　　　Your friend,
　　　　　　　　　　　　Lorne

Dear Dad:
　　Our counselor is an expert.
　　He is an expert in sleeping.

　　　　　　　　　　　　Jimmy

Dear Mom and Dad:
    Yesterday I went to the camp barber.
    His name is Victor and he gave me a nice haircut. I think you will like it.

                              Love,
                              Carl

P.S. The kids call me Baldy now.

Dear Mom and Dad:
    This is a very good camp.
    Nobody ever runs away.
    The guards and the big fence help a lot.

                              Patricia

Dear Folks:
 I am the best swimmer in the whole camp because I am the only one whose bathing suit doesn't fall off.

> Your son,
> Lloyd

Dear Mom and Dad:
 This camp is the perfect place to be if you don't want to have a good time.

> Love,
> Herbert

Dear Mom and Dad:
 I like the camp.
 I call it Camp Prison.

> Your son

Dear Mom and Dad:
   I won the prize at camp for the best costume at the masquerade party.
   Here is a picture of me in my costume.
   You may not recognize me because I am dressed as a man from outer space.

                                    Love,
                                    Stephen

Dear Parents:
   How much money do they pay the counselor?
   They shouldn't pay him much because the counselor doesn't do anything but sleep, eat, and chase kids.

                                    David

Dear Parents:
   I can't write to you every day at camp.
I am too busy hitting home runs.

> Love,
> Dexter

Dear Folks:
   You don't have to send me candy unless you want me to starve to death.

> Your son,
> Nelson

Dear Mom and Dad:
   The food at this camp is great if you're not very hungry.

> Love, Cathy

Dear Cathy:
   How are the boys at your camp?
   The boys at this camp are terrible except for Jimmy, Peter, Martin, Carl, Larry, Bruce, Arnold, Stanley, and Roger.

                              Your girlfriend,
                              Wilma

Dear Folks:
   I would like to come to this camp in the wintertime.
   Then the other kids won't be here.

                              Love,
                              Your son

Dear Folks:
   Please write and tell me if I am having a good time at camp.

>   Love,
>   Your son

Dear Mom:
   The weather at camp is great if you have a raincoat.

>   Love,
>   Diane

Dear Mom and Dad:
   Please write and tell me why I like camp.

>   Love,
>   Jimmy

Dear Grandma:
   Could you send me a watch to camp?
   I want to keep time on how long the counselor sleeps.
   I think it is all day.

> Your granddaughter

Dear Mark:
   I have a new girlfriend at camp.
   Her name is Susan.
   I met her at the camp dance.
   I love her because she is the only girl at the camp dance who didn't step on my feet.

> Your friend,
> Bruce

Dear Folks:
 We have a great cook at camp.
 His best dish is burnt toast.

> Love,
> Marsha

Dear Folks:
 The food at camp is great.
 The best meal is bread and water.

> Arnie

Dear Mom:
 I am fine.
 Today I didn't bleed as much as yesterday.

> Lucy

Dear Mom:
 I don't like this camp.
 They make you take a shower every week even if you're not dirty.

> Love,
> Annie

Dear Mom and Dad:
   The best thing about this camp is the bus ride home.

                              Love,
                              Eileen

Dear Folks:
   Our counselor's name is Murray.
   He likes kids, but not very much.

                              Your son,
                              Michael

Dear Mother:
   Thank you for sending me to this great camp.
   I cry myself to sleep every night.

                              Love,
                              Betsy

Dear Mom and Dad:
 Monday I hit a home run in the baseball game.
 Tuesday I hit a home run in the baseball game.
 Wednesday I hit a home run in the baseball game.
 Thursday I hit a home run in the baseball game.
 Friday I hit a home run in the baseball game.
 I hope we play against the girls' team again next week so I can hit another home run.

Love,
Roger

Dear Parents:
 Our counselor has a great sense of humor. He always laughs before he socks you.

Love,
Harvey

Dear Mom and Dad:
Everybody has the flu at camp except the camp doctor.
He quit!

> Your daughter

Dear Folks:
Our camp baseball team needs a new pitcher, catcher, first baseman, shortstop, manager, and coach.
Everything else is okay.

> Your son

Dear Mom and Dad:
They have a new lifeguard at camp.
The other one couldn't swim.

> Love,
> Theresa

Dear Mother and Father:
    My favorite things at camp are:
        1. Eating
        2. Eating
        3. Eating
        4. Eating
        5. Eating
        6. Eating

                              Love,
                              Betsy

P. S. I am starving to death.

Dear Folks:
    There is a spy in my bunk.
    Somebody told the counselor I didn't brush my teeth today.

                              Your son,
                              George

Dear Sister:
    I miss you.
    Now you know how terrible this camp really is.

>   Your brother,
>   Alfred

Dear Mom and Dad:
    There are six kids in my cabin.
    Everyone is in good health except the five kids that are sick.

>   Your son,
>   Julian

Dear Mom:
    This camp is great if you don't think about it too much.

>   Love,
>   Your son,
>   Arnold

Dear Mom and Dad:
    My best friend at camp is Amy.
    My next best friend at camp is Susie.
    My next, next best friend at camp is Beth.
    My next, next, next best friend at camp is Lois.
    My next, next, next, next best friend at camp is Debbie.

                              Love,
                              Roberta
P.S. I will write you tomorrow with the name of my next, next, next, next, next best friend.

Dear Folks:
    Please send me a lot of rope to camp.
    I am planning my escape.

                              Love,
                              Your son

Dear Mom and Dad:
    Everything is okay at camp if you don't ask too many questions.

                                    Paula

Dear Mom and Dad:
    They give you a lot to eat at the camp if you're on a diet.

                                    Love,
                                    Rita

Dear Grandma:
    Thank you for sending me the chocolate cake.
    The counselor let me have one piece before he ate it.

                                    Love,
                                    Your granddaughter

Dear Mother and Father:
    I am the best baseball player at camp.
    I am the best football player at camp.
    I am the best tennis player at camp.
    I am the best swimmer at camp.
    I am the best basketball player at camp.

Love,
Jimmy

P.S. Don't worry, I won't get a swelled head.

Dear Lloyd:
    What do you like best about your camp?
    The thing I like best about my camp is that it doesn't last too long.

Your friend,
Stacey

Dear Mom and Dad:
 I was voted the most popular kid in my bunk.
 Please send another box of Tootsie Rolls.

> Your daughter,
> Lisa

Dear Dad:
 You would like this camp a lot.
 The counselor likes to sleep till noon just like you.

> Your son,
> Mickey

Dear Mother:
 The camp laundry is very good.
 They send you back your clothes nice and clean even if they aren't yours.

> Love from,
> Susan

Dear Mom and Dad:
    Here are the clothes I need for camp.
    1. Shoes
    2. Socks
    3. Pants
    4. Shirts
    5. Underwear
    6. Jackets
    7. Sweaters
    8. Hankies
I have everything else.

                              Love,
                              Bobby

Dear Mom and Dad:
    I think the camp doctor used to work in a meat market because everybody calls him The Butcher.

                              Naomi

Dear Mom:
   I have the best part in the camp play because I have the loudest voice.

>   Love,
>   Your daughter,
>   Diane

Dear Folks:
   I got sick last night, but don't worry. My best friend, Billy, took care of me.
   He is going to be a doctor when he grows up.

>   Your son

Dear Folks:
   We had a big surprise at camp today.
   The cook didn't burn the food.

>   Love,
>   Allison

Dear Mom and Dad:
    Here are the things I like about camp:
    1. The weather.
    2. The drinking water.
    3. The grass.
    4. The camp dog.

                              Love,
                              Wendy

Dear Mom and Dad:
    Why do I have to write to all my relatives?
    I don't have anything to say except "How are you, I am fine."

                              Love,
                              Marsha

Dear Mother:
　Please send my bike up to camp.
　I am tired of walking on the camp hikes.

　　　　　　　　　　Love,
　　　　　　　　　　David

Dear Mom and Dad:
　I don't like camp.
　They make you have fun even if you don't want to.

　　　　　　　　　　Stephanie

Dear Folks:
　Every day when the sun shines they make you go outside and have a good time.
　I hope it rains soon.

　　　　　　　　　　Love,
　　　　　　　　　　Your daughter

Dear Mom and Dad:
 Here is a picture of my best friend at camp.
 His name is Arnie.
 Please rip up the picture of my best friend that I sent you last week.
 I am not talking to him anymore.

> Love,
> Stephen

Dear Grandma:
 I hope you can come up and visit me at camp so I can show you all the places I hate here.
 I am having a wonderful time.

> Your grandson,
> Mike

Dear Mom:
    We had a pillow fight in the bunk.
    I won because I put a shoe in my pillow.

Love,
Jerry

Dear Dad:
    Please send a life preserver right away.
    I sink in the swimming pool.

Herbie

Dear Folks:
    Today they gave us steak for supper.
    They must have made a mistake.

Perry

Dear Mom:
    Camp is lots of fun.
    We all have nicknames.
    I am prisoner 46.

                              Love,
                              Billy

Dear Brother:
    You would like this camp a lot.
    None of the kids like to take a bath.

                              Your brother,
                              Anthony

Dear Folks:
    This camp must be very cheap.
    Yesterday I heard the counselor say he wouldn't give two cents for it.

                              Your son,
                              Nelson

Dear Father:
    We have a lot of fun on rainy days at camp.
    We hold buckets under the holes in the roof.

                              Your son,
                              Morton

Dear Folks:
    Our football team lost five games at camp.
    I think our football team needs a new coach, but we can't get a new coach because our coach is Peter and his father paid for the football uniforms.

Your son,
Barry

Dear Grandma:
    I hope you can come up to camp on visiting day.
    You don't have to bring any presents.

Love,
Cara

P.S. My mother made me write this letter.

Dear Mom and Dad:
    Please send me a new pair of sneakers.
    The sneakers I have came in last in the race today.

                                    Love,
                                    Jimmy

Dear Mom:
    Yesterday was a special day at camp.
    The counselor didn't yell at us all day.

                                    Love,
                                    Jerry

Dear Parents:
    I am fine.
    Please send a box of bandages and aspirin.

                                    Love,
                                    Gwen

Dear Mom and Dad:
 I am fine.
 How are you?
 Last week we played tennis, went swimming, went on a hike, saw a movie, had a campfire, went to a carnival, saw a circus and went to a play. I am bored.

> Love,
> Babs

Dear Folks:
 I can't write home every day. My hand is getting tired.
 Please send me $5 in coins so I can call home instead.

> Love,
> Mary Ellen

Dear Grandparents:
 Please send me some candy.
 They don't give you anything at camp except regular food.

>   Your grandson,
>   Arnie

Dear Mom and Dad:
 The sports I hate at camp are tennis, swimming, and baseball.
 I like all the rest.

>   Love,
>   Caroline

Dear Mom and Dad:
 Please send me my rabbit's foot to camp.
 I need a lot of luck up here.

>   Love,
>   Cynthia

Dear Folks:
　　Monday our baseball team lost.
　　Tuesday our football team lost.
　　Wednesday our basketball team lost.
　　Thursday our swimming team lost.
　　Friday our hockey team lost.
　　Next week I want to go to another camp.

　　　　　　　　　　　　　　　Franklin

Dear Folks:
　　Don't worry, I have plenty of clothes.
　　My friend, Lewis, sold me his underwear for 25 cents.

　　　　　　　　　　　　　　Your son,
　　　　　　　　　　　　　　Nicholas

Dear Folks:
    We have the best counselor in the camp because he never hits the kids on Sunday.

                                Your son,
                                Ronald

Dear Folks:
    Please bring Skipper to camp on visiting day.
    He would like it here because this camp is a real dog's life.

                                Love,
                                William

Dear Uncle Herb:
    Help!

                                Love,
                                Your nephew
                                at camp,
                                Mark

Dear Mom and Dad:
    Monday we had spaghetti for dinner.
    Tuesday we had spaghetti for dinner.
    Wednesday we had spaghetti for dinner.
    Thursday we had spaghetti for dinner.
    Friday we had spaghetti for dinner.
    I think the cook at camp is Italian.

                                      Love,
                                      Richard

Dear Susan:
    I met a boy at camp.
    I think I love him.
    I will write you more after I find out his name.

                                  Your girlfriend,
                                  Barbara

Dear Mom and Dad:
   The thing we like about camp best is when we go to sleep.

                              Love,
                              Patricia

Dear Parents:
   Thank you for sending me to camp.
   I would like to come to this camp again, but not too soon.

                              Harvey

Dear Mom and Dad:
   Please save my letters from camp so I can remember what a terrible time I had.

                              Your son,
                              Eric

Dear Dad:
    Thank you for sending me to camp.
    I know it cost a lot of money.
    When I grow up, I will send my son to camp someday even if he doesn't want to like me.

                                    Your son,
                                    Arnie

Dear Mom and Dad:
    All the kids at camp like me a lot except the ones that I socked last week.

                                    Your son,
                                    Gabriel

Dear Folks:
   We share everything at camp.
   Last week my best friend, Myrna, shared her poison ivy with me.

                              Love,
                              Stella

Dear Dad:
   I am the captain of my baseball team at camp because I am the only one with my own bat and ball.

                              Your son,
                              Roger

Dear Mother and Father:
   Everybody thinks the food is great at camp except the kids who like to eat.

                              Love,
                              Ivan

Dear Folks:
   You have to go to bed at 9 o'clock at camp and you have to change your clothes once a week and brush your teeth and wash your face.
   Next year, I want to go to another camp where they let you have fun.

>   Love,
>   Patricia

Dear Parents:
   Why do I have to write a letter home every day?
   There isn't anything to say but hello and goodbye.

>   Love,
>   Marsha

Dear Folks:
My counselor is ten feet tall.

                                    Richie

Dear Mommy:
The food gives me a tummy ache so I stopped eating.
Bye.

                                    Beth

Dear Dad:
Are you sure Mickey Mantle got his start at a camp like this?

                                Your son,
                                Marlon

Dear Folks:
 The counselor taught me how to swim underwater. First he holds my head down.

                                        Mickey

Dear Mom and Dad:
You have to make your bed every day at camp.
I am sleeping on the floor.

Debbie

Dear Ray:
I was the highest scorer in the big basketball game last week.
My brother, Philip, was the scorekeeper.

Your friend,
Bobby

Dear Folks:
I got the award for the cleanest kid in the bunk this week because I was the only kid who took a bath.

Your son,
Victor

Dear Parents:
   They wrote a big story about me in the camp newspaper.
   Ellen is the editor of the camp paper and she only charged me $2 for the story because she is my best friend.

> Your daughter,
> Aileen

Dear Mother and Father:
   You sure learn a lot at this camp.
   Yesterday they taught us how to put out the fire in the bunk.

> Love,
> Cynthia

Dear Mom and Dad:
    I am having a wonderful time.
    Please send me my bus ticket home.

                                        Susan

Dear Mom and Dad:
    This is the best camp in the whole world.
    The counselor told me so yesterday.

                                        Love,
                                        Charles

Dear Folks:
    There are lots of things I like about camp and I will write you as soon as I think what they are.

                                        Your son,
                                        Bruce

Dear Grandpa:
    Did you go to camp when you were a little boy?
    Which camp did you go to?
    Did you like camp?
    Please send me the name of your camp.
    I would like to go there next year even if it is a real old camp.

                                    Duane

Dear Folks:
    I hope I can come back to this camp again next summer.

                                  Your son,
                                  Denny

P.S. My counselor said I had to write this letter.

Dear Mom:
 I will brush my teeth every day at camp as soon as I find my toothbrush.

Susan

Dear Grandma:
 The counselor has taught us a lot.
 Yesterday he taught us how to smoke in bed.

Dennis

Dear Mom:
 We have a pet frog.
 He is the cleanest one in the bunk.

Jeffrey

Dear Mom and Dad:
    This camp is the best thing that ever happened to me since I was born.

                                Love,
                                Roger

P.S. I hope things get better when I get older.

Dear Jimmy:
    I am captain of the baseball team at camp.
    I had to pay 24 Johnny Bench picture cards to get the job.

                                Your pal,
                                Alvin

Dear Mom and Dad:
   I am the best tennis player in the whole camp because I am the only one with my own racket.

                              Love,
                              Stephanie

Dear Folks:
   I am eating good at camp like you told me.
   Yesterday I ate two Hershey bars, 3 cokes and a box of popcorn.

                              Phyllis

Dear Mom and Dad:
   The new counselor is very nice, but he doesn't talk too much except to say shut up.

                              Love,
                              Charlie

Dear Joan:
    How are the boys at your camp?
    The boys at my camp are better than the boys at my camp last year, but not as good as the boys at my camp the year before last year.

Your friend,
Pearl

Dear Mom and Dad:
    Our counselor is very smart.
    He can watch us swimming even when he is sleeping at the lake.

Love,
Your daughter

Dear Mom and Dad:
    I want to thank you for sending me to camp, but not much.

                           Your son,
                           Carlton

Dear Folks:
    I haven't lost any clothes at camp because I haven't changed my clothes since we got here.

                           Love,
                           Carol

Dear Mother and Father:
    Everybody likes to swim in the camp lake, even the water snakes.

                           Your son,
                           Arnold

Dear Aaron:
    Thank you for your letter.
    Your camp sounds great.
    I would write you all about my camp, but I am trying to forget.

                                Your friend,
                                Neil

Dear Mom and Dad:
    I am not homesick anymore.

                                Love,
                                Stephanie
P.S. Yesterday was the last time I cried all day.

Dear Folks:
   We go to church every Sunday at camp and we all say our prayers that next summer will be better.

>   Your daughter,
>   Cynthia

Dear Mom and Dad:
   Our counselor said we were the best kids he ever had at camp.
   Yesterday he quit.

>   Love,
>   Walter

Dear Mom and Dad:
   The flowers are beautiful at camp, especially the poison ivy.

>   Love,
>   Junior

Dear Folks:
 I hit a home run in the baseball game.
 Next week the pitcher said he will let me hit another home run if I give him another box of bubble gum.

>   Your son,
>   Larry

Dear Jimmy:
 I hope you are having a good time at your camp.
 I am having a good time at my camp.

>   Your pal,
>   Jeff

P.S. I hate this place.

Dear Folks:
 Our new counselor is very nice.
 He always shares the candy and cookies we get from home with us.

                    Love,
                    Peter

Dear Mom and Dad:
 I swam across the lake all by myself.
 It was a lot of fun except I almost sank twice.

                    Love,
                    Sharon

Dear Sandra:
 Please come to my camp next summer.
 I will share my boyfriend with you.

                    Your friend,
                    Carole

Dear Mom and Dad:
    Camp is great.
    Everything is okay.

                                      Love,
                                      Andy

P.S. What is an epidemic?

Dear Mom and Dad:
   My counselor is my hero.
   He told me so.

                              Love,
                              Bruce

Dear Daddy:
   My favorite flower at camp is poison ivy.

                              Tina

Dear Teacher:
   You would like my counselor.
   He hates kids too.

                              Your pupil,
                              Paul

Dear Mother and Father:
    Monday it rained.
    Tuesday it rained.
    Wednesday it rained.
    Thursday it rained.
    Friday it rained.
    Saturday it rained.
    Sunday it rained.

                                      Love,
                                      Gwen
P. S. It was the best week at camp.

Dear Jimmy:
    Our counselor is lazy, selfish, dirty and a liar.
    But nobody is perfect.

                                      Your friend,
                                      Nicholas

Dear Mom:
    I am fine, but don't ask me how I am feeling.

Love,
Betsy

Dear Aunt Jennifer:
    The only people who eat good at this camp are the mosquitos.
    They eat everybody.

Your niece

Dear Mom:
    I miss your cooking at camp.
    They don't have burnt toast.

Love,
Aileen

Dear Parents:
   My favorite game at camp is called "fool the counselor."
   We played the game once, but I don't think we will be able to play it again.

>   Your son,
>   Foster

Dear Mom and Dad:
   My best friend at camp is Selma.
   We share everything except my boyfriend.

>   Love,
>   Brenda

Dear Mother:
   Our counselor is very nice.
   Every night before we go to sleep, he reads us another story from Playboy Magazine.

>   Your son,
>   Mike

Dear Parents:
   I am having a good time at camp.
   Please send me the name of my camp.
   I forgot again.

>   Love,
>   Jean

Dear Mother and Father:
   I threw up last night.
   Nothing else is new.

>   Marilyn

Dear Mom and Dad:
   We went mountain climbing and everybody had a good time except the kid that had to carry the counselor's pack up the mountain.
   That was me.

>   Love,
>   William

P. S. It wasn't so bad because the counselor carried his pack down the mountain.

Dear Folks:
   We had a campfire at camp last night.
   All the kids had a good time except the two kids that got hurt in the fire.

>   Love,
>   Ira

Dear Mom and Dad:
   I am having a wonderful time.
   I want to come home.

                              Love,
                              Stevie

Dear Parents:
   The counselor said I am the best boy in the whole bunch.
   Please give the counselor a big tip.

                              Lloyd

Dear Parents:
   Do counselors have any brains?
   My friend Bobby and I would like to know.

                              Archie

Dear Mom and Dad:
    Monday our baseball team lost 10 to 0.
    Tuesday our baseball team lost 12 to 0.
    Wednesday our baseball team lost 14 to 0.
    Thursday our baseball team lost 9 to 0.
    Friday our baseball team lost 20 to 0.
    Our baseball team hopes we get rained out tomorrow.

                                Your son,
                                Skippy

Dear Grandpa:
    We have a pet dog in our bunk at camp.
    His name is Mickey and he barks at the counselor all day.

                                Gilda

Dear Mom and Dad:
    I don't think my counselor likes me anymore. He hasn't socked me all week.

                              Your son,
                              Jay

Dear Father:
    This camp is very poor.
    They can't afford a watch dog, so they have a watch cat.

                              Bernice

Dear Mother:
    I miss you and Dad very much.
    Nobody yells at me at camp.

                              Your daughter

Dear Mom and Dad:
  Here are the things I don't like about camp:
  1. The food
  2. The sports
  3. The kids
  4. The counselor
  5. The bunks
  6. The head counselor
  7. The weather
  I will write you the things I like about the camp as soon as I think of something.

  Love,
  Stephanie

Dear Mom and Dad:
  This camp is a lot of fun if you don't expect too much.

  Nancy

Dear Mom and Dad:
    The counselor is pregnant.
    Nothing else is new.

                                Love,
                                Babs

Dear Folks:
    Please don't ask me about the food at camp.
    I am trying not to think about it.

                                Love,
                                Rebecca

Dear Daddy:
    We found a skunk in the bunk.
    We named him after the counselor.

                                Love,
                                Andy

Dear Folks:
    Monday we had franks and beans.
    Tuesday we had franks and sauerkraut.
    Wednesday we had franks and spaghetti.
    Thursday we had franks and potato chips.
    Friday we had franks and pickles.
    Saturday we had franks and soda.
    I think they can buy franks very cheap here.

                                    Love,
                                    Harriet

Dear Parents:
    I had a dream last night, but my dream didn't come true. When I woke up I was still at camp.

                                    Your son

Dear Mom and Dad:
   The best day at camp hasn't happened yet. It is the last day.

                    Love,
                    Olga

Dear Parents:
   My favorite place at camp is the infirmary. I have been there more times than anybody.

                    Lee

Dear Grandparents:
   This camp is very pretty. Especially at night when they throw the garbage away.

                    Love,
                    Karl

Dear Folks:
    The food at camp is great.
    The best is the bread and water.

                                Your daughter,
                                Bernice

Dear Mom and Dad:
    I don't like this camp.
    They won't let me play my records all day.

                        Your daughter,
                        Aileen

Dear Folks:
    Please write me right away and tell me if I like camp.

                        Love,
                        Paula

Dear Grandparents:
    Please send me $10.
    I want to bribe the counselor not to sock me for one week.

                        Your grandson,
                        Wally

Dear Grandparents:
   Please send me some food from home.
   Send anything.
   Even a few crumbs will be better than what we get here.

   Love,
   Your grand-
   daughter

Dear Mom and Dad:
   We play a lot of games at camp.
   My favorite game is hide and seek.
   Last week we played hide and seek and Jimmy hid and it was two days before they found him.

   Love,
   Robert

Dear Mommy:
   I am not homesick anymore.
   Now I have the chicken pox.

> Your daughter,
> Annie

Dear Mom and Dad:
   Camp is a fun place to be if you don't know any better.

> Gretchen

Dear Dad:
   I am glad you sent me to camp, but I am not sure I know why.

> Your daughter,
> Stephanie

Dear Mom and Dad:
 At 9:00, we had tennis.
 At 9:30, we had baseball.
 At 10:00, we had soccer.
 At 10:30, we had football.
 At 11:00, we had swimming.
 At 1:00, we had softball.
 At 1:30, we had basketball.
 At 2:45, we had arts and crafts.
 At 3:00, we had the camp play.
 This place is a gyp. There isn't anything to do.

           Martin

Dear Folks:
 This camp is a gyp.
 They don't even have color television in our tent.

           Your daughter,
           Viola

Dear Mom:
 I broke my leg.
 I am learning to walk on my other leg.

> Your son,
> Chic

Dear Folks:
 Yesterday we played a joke on our counselor.
 We put a frog in his bed and he laughed after he socked us.

> Your son,
> James

Dear Teacher:
 I miss you and all the other teachers at school and I hope the summer lasts forever.

> Your student,
> Aaron

Dear Mom and Dad:
    Monday I had a cold.
    Tuesday I had a headache.
    Wednesday I had a stomach ache.
    Thursday I sprained my ankle.
    Friday I broke my finger.
    Saturday I cut my hand.
    Sunday was okay.

                                Love,
                                Holly

Dear Folks:
    I am not afraid of the counselor anymore.

                                Love,
                                Rex
P.S. Except when he gets mad.

Dear Daddy:
　Please don't send me any N.Y. Mets baseball scores.
　They are ruining my summer vacation.

　　　　　　　　　　　Your son

Dear Mom and Dad:
　The counselor is very neat.
　He makes us eat with a knife and fork.

　　　　　　　　　　　Love,
　　　　　　　　　　　Teddy

Dear Aunt Judy:
　I sure had good luck to get to go to this camp.
　Next summer I hope I have better luck and get to stay at home.

　　　　　　　　　　　Wally

Dear Aunt Ruth:
 I like camp a lot.
 Here is a picture of me at camp.
 The kid next to me in the picture is smiling because he is going home tomorrow.

> Your nephew,
> Philip

Dear Mom and Dad:
 There are 300 comic books in the camp library.
 I like the camp library better than my school library.

> Your son

Dear Dad:
 I am the fastest runner at camp.
 I learned to run fast when the counselor chases me.

> Your son,
> Aaron

Dear Parents:
 I am having a very good time at camp and yesterday I laughed for the first time.

> Your daughter,
> Babs

Hi Dad:
 Guess what!
 I've been at camp for twelve days and so far I haven't broken anything.

> Love,
> Jerry

Dear Naomi:
   How do you like your camp?
   I hate my camp except for one boy who I love.
   His name is David and he is very good looking in a funny sort of way.

                              Your friend,
                              Amy

Dear Susan:
   Here is the picture of my boyfriend at camp.
   He isn't so good looking, but he's the only boyfriend I've got.

                              Yours truly,
                              Lois

Dear Lois:
 I met a great boy at the camp dance.
 He hates to dance like me.

>Your friend,
>Natalie

Dear Dad:
 I struck out six times in the baseball game.
 Next summer I want to go to another camp where the pitchers aren't so good.

>Mickey

Dear Mom and Dad:
 They fired the camp doctor.
 They found out he doesn't like sick kids.

>Love,
>Harrison

Dear Parents:
   Everything is great at camp, but we need a new umpire for the baseball game.
   The umpire we have is too fair and we can never win with a fair umpire.

>   Your son,
>   Franklin

Dear Mom and Dad:
   I got your letter and the answer to your question is that I have been washing my hands every day even if I am not in the mood.

>   Love,
>   Sarah

Dear Mom and Dad:
    The toilet broke again.
    You sort of get used to the woods.

                              Love,
                              Kenny

Dear Larry:
    There are ten kids on our baseball team at camp and they all play first base.

                            Your friend,
                            Randy

Dear Aunt Sarah and Uncle Milton:
    I like the camp a lot.
    I wish I were dead.

                            Your nephew,
                            Stuart

Dear Mom and Dad,
    There is a thief in my bunk. Somebody stole my soap.
    I will wash when I get home.

                                Love,
                                Marty

Dear Mom and Dad:
  Yesterday I went out in a rowboat.
  The boat sank and so did I.

                              Love,
                              Rhoda

Dear Mom and Dad:
  Last night we slept in the woods.
  Nobody was scared except the counselor.

                              Marc

Dear Folks:
  Today was a lot of fun.
  The counselor let me make his bed, give him breakfast in bed, and row him across the lake.

                              Debbie

Dear Evan:
    I am the new pitcher for our camp baseball team.
    The other pitcher quit because he couldn't strike anybody out.

                            Your friend,
                            Abe

P. S. I don't think he could strike anybody out because he closed his eyes when he pitched the ball.

Dear Mother and Father:
    The food is great.
    Today I had stale bread.

                            Amy

Dear Mom and Dad:
 Everybody at camp is having a great time except the kids that didn't run away.

> Your daughter,
> Marilyn

Dear Folks:
 I am in good health and the doctor says I will be better after he operates.

> Your son,
> Jay

Hi Parents:
 I miss my room at home.
 My bunk at camp is too clean.

> Love,
> James

Dear Mother and Father:
We have a new pet in our bunk, but I don't know how long we can keep him because the counselor said he really doesn't like skunks.

>   Love,
>   Christopher

Dear Folks:
The ride up to camp this year was better than last year.
None of the kids got sick except the bus driver.

>   Your daughter,
>   Jane

Dear Folks:
 I miss my brother and sister at camp because there is nobody to fight with at camp except the counselor and he is too big.

>Your son,
>Benny

Dear Uncle Samuel:
 This is my third summer at this camp and I am going to keep coming back until I like it.

>Your nephew,
>Hillel

Dear Folks:
 The water is very clean since they stopped letting the kids go to the bathroom in the swimming pool.

>Love,
>Billy

Dear Mom:
    I received your last letter and don't worry I won't break any bones at camp this summer like I did last summer.
    I found out a way to make sure I can't break anything.
    I stay in bed all day.

                          Your son,
                          Charles

Dear Folks:
    I am okay, but I have a summer cold.
    But don't worry. At least, I don't have a winter cold.

                          Love,
                          Your daughter

Dear Mom and Dad:
　　Please don't send any more soap to me at camp.
　　Nobody uses it here.

　　　　　　　　　　　　Love,
　　　　　　　　　　　　Diane

Dear Dad:
　　Thank you for sending me the new baseball bat.
　　Yesterday I got two hits.
　　I think the new bat is a better hitter.

　　　　　　　　　　　　Paul

Dear Teacher:
　　Do you miss school?
　　I miss school and I hope the summer lasts forever.

　　　　　　　　　　　　Your pupil,
　　　　　　　　　　　　Billy

Dear Mother and Father:
    Please send my rock and roll music up to camp.
    They don't have any loud music here and I can't think without my rock and roll music.

Love,
Laura

Dear Mom and Dad:
    Everybody hates the camp bugler.
    He wakes you up every morning at 7:00.

Love,
Denise

P. S. Except the counselor. She never gets up until after we serve her breakfast in bed.

Dear Mom and Dad:
 The camp laundry lost my underwear, three shirts, four pair of pants, ten socks and my new jacket.
 I got everything else.

       Your son

Dear Mom:
 Everybody likes the counselor, even the two kids that ran away.

       Love,
       Mickey

Dear Raymond:
 I am going to keep coming back to this camp next year and the year after until I have a good time.

       Your friend,
       Burton

Dear Mom and Dad:
 We have a new nickname for the camp counselor.
 We can't use the old nickname anymore because the counselor said he would wash out our mouths with soap and water.

                          Love,
                          Pauline

Dear Folks:
 I don't like the counselor.
 I don't like the food.
 I don't like the kids in my bunk.
 I am having lots of fun.

                          Randy

Dear Mother and Father:
    We had boxing at camp today and I fought the kid with the knockout punch.

                      Your son,
                      Eddie

Dear Mom and Dad:
    We have a new counselor.
    I can't tell you what he looks like because he has a beard.

                      Love,
                      Billy

Dear Aunt Shirley:
    We had a funeral at camp yesterday.
    Our pet mouse died.

                      Love,
                      Your nephew

Dear Betsy:
  Could I please borrow a dress from you for the camp dance?
  I only have jeans and they don't let you dance in jeans at this camp.
  They are very old-fashioned.

> Lois

Dear Bobby:
  Here is a picture of me at camp.
  The kid standing next to me is Stanley, my very best friend at camp.
  He isn't smiling because I just socked him.

> Your pal,
> Jack

Dear Mom and Dad:
 I can't write to you again for a few weeks.
 I am in training for the big football game.

>   Love,
>   Your son

Dear Mother:
 Please send my dog to camp.
 I have nobody to talk to here.

>   Love,
>   Vicki

Hi Folks:
 I don't like this camp much except for baseball, basketball, football, swimming, tennis, hockey, golf and soccer.

>   Your son,
>   Stuart

Dear Mom and Dad,
    Every day at meal-time we say our prayers that we can get at the steak before the counselor does.

                                    Love,
                                    Billy

Dear Mom:
This camp isn't like the camp I went to last summer.
They like kids here.

> Your daughter,
> Marsha

Dear Mom and Dad:
I will write you about all the good news at camp as soon as something good happens.

> Your son,
> Daniel

Dear Mom and Dad:
The best thing about the basketball game at camp is the time out.

> Your son,
> Danny

Dear Grandparents:
 Please don't cry when you see me at camp.

                    Love,
                    Susie
P.S. You can cry when you get home from seeing me at camp.

Dear Jennifer:
 How are the boys at your camp?
 The boys at my camp are terrible and I love three of them.

                    Your girl-
                    friend,
                    Natalie

Dear Dad:
 I hope you are having a nice summer.
 I miss my allowance.

       Jonathan

Dear Mom and Dad:
 Our counselor is very clean.
 He always washes his hands before he socks us.

       Your son

Dear Folks:
 Everybody in the bunk made a wish and if our wish comes true next week, we will have a new counselor.

       Your son

Dear Folks:
　　Our counselor tells us a story every night at camp.
　　He likes to tell us scary stories and sometimes we don't sleep so good.

　　　　　　　　　　　Love,
　　　　　　　　　　　Frederick

Dear Mom and Dad:
　　My best friend at camp is Jimmy.
　　I like Jimmy a lot.
　　We do lots of things together like put snakes in the counselor's bed.

　　　　　　　　　　　Love,
　　　　　　　　　　　Kenny

Dear Teacher:
  I am having a good time at camp.
  I hope you have a good summer and come back to school in a good mood.

>   Your student,
>   Frances

Dear Folks:
  The food at camp is very good.
  My favorite meal is leftovers.

>   Love,
>   Morton

Dear Mom and Dad:
  We have a great tennis counselor at camp.
  She knows a lot about tennis.
  She once watched Billy Jean King play.

>   Your daughter

Dear Grandma:
 Could you please bake me a chocolate cake and send it to me at camp?
 Please write *Secret* on the package so I can eat the chocolate cake before the other kids get it.

 Your grandson,
 Jayson

Dear Noel:
 Here is a picture of the girls at my camp.
 Could you send me a picture of the girls at your camp so I can see if I want to go to your camp next summer?

 Your buddy,
 Arnold

Dear Grandpa:
I eat a lot at camp, but don't worry, I am not getting fat because I throw up a lot too.

> Your granddaughter,
> Jane

Dear Grandma:
Camp is better this year than last year.
Last year they had a black and white television.
This year they have a color television set.

> Love,
> Your grandson

Dear Parents:
They have nice trees at camp.
My dog would like it up here.

> Love,
> Sidney

Dear Iris:
 I gained six pounds at camp.
 How much weight did you gain?
 If you didn't gain any weight, please don't write and tell me about it.

> Your friend,
> Janet

Dear Folks:
 Remember last summer when I broke my left arm?
 Guess what just happened to my right arm?

> Love,
> Mickey

Dear Folks:
   This is my first day at camp.
   I am happy because soon it will be my last day at camp.

                              Heloise

Dear Mom and Dad:
   Someday I would like to come back to this camp as a counselor so I can get even.

                              Love,
                              Bertha

Dear Mom and Dad:
   I learned how to swim underwater.
   It was easy after Freddy pushed my head underwater.

                              Your son,
                              George

Dear Bonnie:
   There aren't any good-looking boys at my camp.
   Can I borrow a boy from your camp for our next camp dance?

                              Love,
                              Bella

Dear Bruce:
   I hope I see you at the next camp dance.
   Do you hope you see me?

                              Love,
                              Susan

P. S. You don't have to answer.
P.P.S. I hope you do.

Dear Teacher:
   I am learning a lot at camp.
   Today I learned how to cut a dead snake in little pieces.

                              Your pupil,
                              Manuel

Dear Mom and Dad:
   My counselor is just like my brother, Wendell. He is a pain.

                              Your son,
                              Aaron

Dear Aunt Molly:
   There are a lot of nice kids at camp, even the ones I am not talking to anymore.

                              William

Dear Parents:
   I got a haircut at camp.
   My best friend, Stevie, did it for nothing.

                        Love,
                        Bernie
P.S. The regular barber charges $2.50.

Dear Parents:
   Why do you want me to write home every week?
   I thought you didn't like to get bad news.

                        Your son,
                        Art

Dear Mom and Dad:
   I am not afraid of the water anymore.
   It helped a lot when the counselor pushed me in.

>   Your son

Dear Folks:
   Please send me some food from home.
   Anything.
   I am desperate.

>   Mickey

Dear Folks:
   They make you have a good time at camp even if you don't want to.

>   Love,
>   Your son

Hi Folks,
 Please send me a picture of measles, poison ivy, chicken pox and the mumps. I got something and I want to find out what it is.

Your daughter,
Diane Paula

Dear Barry:
    I would like to borrow your baseball glove.
    My baseball glove made three errors in the game today.

                              Your buddy,
                              Franklin

Dear Parents:
    Please bring your automobile when you come to see me at camp.
    I need a getaway car.

                              Love,
                              Sally

Dear Grandma:
    I miss you and Grandpa very much.
    Please send a few dollars so I won't forget you.

                              Your grandson,
                              Arnold

Dear Grandma and Grandpa:
   Tomorrow is my birthday at camp and for my birthday present the kids in the bunk said they wouldn't sock me for the whole day.

>   Love,
>   Veronica

Dear Mom and Dad:
   I think the counselor really likes me better than anyone.
   He said I have the best toilet habits in the whole bunk.

>   Jimmy

Dear Dad:
 I have a new girlfriend at camp.
 Her name is Kim.
 She hates her counselor, too.

>   Love,
>   Fredrick

Dear Folks:
 The weather is very nice at camp.
 It only rains during the day.

>   Your daughter,
>   Marsha

Dear Folks:
 I have a surprise when I come home from camp.
 I am bringing all of my dirty laundry with me.

>   Love,
>   Alvin

Dear Roger:
  We need a first baseman for our camp baseball team.
  We also need a catcher, a second baseman, a short stop and a third baseman.
  We already have eight pitchers.

Your pal,
Noel

Dear Mom and Dad:
  Please make sure you come on parents' visiting day.
  That's the only time they give you a decent meal.

Your son

Dear Uncle Henny:
    Thank you for sending me the candy.
    I traded it with my friend for a better kind.

                                Your nephew,
                                Quincey

Dear Mother and Father:
    We have three rabbits, two frogs, four snakes, and twelve butterflies in our bunk.
    The other kids call our bunk The Zoo.

                                Annie

Dear Folks:
    I think the mosquitos really like me.
    I have more bites than anybody.

                                Love,
                                Darlene

Dear Mom and Dad:
 Baseball is terrible at camp and so is tennis, swimming, hockey, basketball, baseball and soccer.
 I am having a wonderful time.

                        Love,
                        Bruce

Dear Angela:
 All the girls talk about at this camp is boys, boys, boys and boys.
 What a great camp.

                      Your friend,
                      Stephanie

Dear Folks:
   There are a lot of things that I like about camp and I will write and tell you as soon as I think of one.

>   Love,
>   Lillian

Dear Folks:
   The counselor gave me a nice present for my birthday.
   He let me make his bed and wash his socks.

>   Love,
>   Roland

Dear Parents:
   You have to eat fast at camp if you want to get the food before the counselor eats it.

>   Love,
>   Johnny

Dear Mom and Dad:
 I like baseball better than basketball and I like swimming better than track and I like soccer better than football.
 But I love lunch and dinner best of all.

> Your son,
> Arnie

Dear Father:
 Thank you for sending me to camp.
 I hope you have a good year in the stock market again so I can come back to camp next summer.

> Love,
> Sylvia

Dear Parents:
   Please send me a picture of my room at home.
   I want to show my counselor that I am not a slob at home too.

                              Love,
                              Denise

Dear Grandma:
   Everybody likes this camp, especially the kids who don't know any better.

                              Your grand-
                              daughter,
                              Felicia

Dear Parents:
   I don't like the movies at this camp.
   There aren't any rated R.

                              Love,
                              Michael

Dear Mom and Dad:
   We took a vote and the most popular person in the bunk wasn't the counselor.

> Your daughter,
> Andrea

P.S. The counselor came in last.

Dear Grandma and Grandpa:
   All the kids in my bunk are very nice except the ones I am not talking to and the ones that I hate.

> Your grand-
> daughter,
> Stephanie

Dear Mom and Dad:
 You don't have to worry.
 There aren't any roaches at this camp like the camp I went to last year.
 The rats ate them all.

                              Jay

Dear Dad:
 I am learning a lot at camp.
 Yesterday my friend taught me how to catch a football and he only charged me two dollars.

                    Your son,
                    Nathan

Dear Parents:
 Yesterday was a special day at camp.
 Everybody took a bath.

                    Love,
                    Janet

Dear Parents:
    A lot of the kids at camp got the measles, but don't worry. I didn't get the measles because you can't get the measles when you have the chicken pox.

                            Love,
                            Stephanie

Dear Folks:
    This camp is much better than the camp I went to last year.
    They give you meat once a week even if you aren't hungry.

                            Your son,
                            Bruce

Dear Mom:
The kids in the bunk wrote a new camp song, but the counselor won't let us sing it because of some of the words.

                        Love,
                        Cynthia

Dear Folks:
Do you have to be smart to be a counselor?

                        Love,
                        Harvey

P.S. My counselor doesn't know I wrote this letter.

Dear Parents:
Please send me all the news from home, but don't send me any bad news.
We have enough bad news up here already.

                        Your son,
                        Sidney

Dear Folks:
 Last night we had the camp play.
 The name of the camp play was The Pied Piper.
 I had the best part.
 I was one of the rats.

> Your son,
> Walter

Dear Ann:
 My boyfriend at camp is the captain of the football team.
 The captain of the football team last week was my boyfriend last week.

> Mary

Dear Parents:
 This camp is terrible.
 I'll bet President Carter would never send Amy here.

>   Your daughter,
>   Lois

Dear Jeff:
 Your new girlfriend sounds great.
 I would like to meet her someday when you don't need her anymore.

>   Your pal,
>   Paul

Dear Judy:
 I kissed a boy at the camp dance.
 I don't know his name, but he was a good kisser.

>   Your friend,
>   Sally

Dear Mom and Dad:
   Remember those nonbreakable glasses the man at the eyeglass store sold us before I left for camp? Well, they are not nonbreakable.

                              Love,
                              Gwen

Dear Dad:
   They really teach you how to play tennis good at camp.
   Next summer they are going to teach me how to hit the ball over the net.

                              Richard

Dear Uncle Martin:
　The food is great at this camp.
　I already lost eight pounds and I have only been here six days.

　　　　　　　　　　Your niece,
　　　　　　　　　　Norma

Dear Folks:
　We won the award for the cleanest bunk in camp because we were the only bunk without cockroaches.
　You will love my camp.

　　　　　　　　　　Your son,
　　　　　　　　　　Nelson

Dear Mom and Dad:
　The food at camp is very good.
　Next summer I want to go to camp near a MacDonald's.

　　　　　　　　　　Love,
　　　　　　　　　　Nan

Dear Folks:
 I hope this camp didn't cost a lot of money.

> Your son,
> Franklin

P. S. I am eating 2nd and 3rd helpings for breakfast, lunch and dinner so you will get your money's worth.

Dear Mother and Father:
 How are you?
 I am fine.
 There is nothing exciting to write about except the fire at the camp.

> Love,
> Richard

Dear Mom and Dad:
> We went on a five-mile hike at camp today.
> It was a lot of fun and I hope we do it again, but not too soon.

>> Love,
>> Roger

Dear Mom and Dad:
> Please send me the key for my camp trunk.
> I have been here two weeks and I am still wearing my city clothes.

>> Love,
>> Irving

Dear Jerry:
> How do you like your camp so far?
> So far this camp is terrible, but I think it will get worse.

>> Your pal,
>> Marc

Dear Mom and Dad:
 The camp play was great.
 Everybody liked it a lot and they said I was the best actor in the play because I was the only one who remembered lines.

                                Love,
                                Arnold

Dear Alvin:
 What kind of camp uniform do you have?
 We have a great camp uniform.
 All the kids wear a torn T-shirt and dirty sneakers.

                              Your friend,
                              Winston

Dear Grandma and Grandpa:
All the kids at this camp are here for the first time.
Nobody ever comes to this camp for the second time.

> Love,
> Daniel

Hi Folks!
The new cook at camp is better than the old cook
I think the new cook knows how to boil water.

> Your daughter,
> Lucy

Dear Jerry:
What is the name of your counselor?
Our counselor's name is Harvey, but everyone calls him The Fink.

> Your buddy,
> Neal

Dear Mother:
  Thank you for sending me to camp.
  I hope you think of something better next summer.

> Your daughter,
> Mona

Dear Mom and Dad:
  You don't have to worry.
  There aren't any more fires at camp since the counselor stopped smoking in bed.

> Your son,
> Bruce

Dear Wilma:
Your new boyfriend at camp sounds great.
I will write you all about my new boyfriend at camp as soon as I find one.

>Your girlfriend,
>Stephanie

Dear Betsy:
We had a camp dance and all the boys were goofy, silly, stupid and a pain.
I can't wait for the next dance.

>Your girlfriend,
>Karen

Dear Mom and Dad:
Why did you send me to this camp?
What did I do wrong?
I promise not to do it again.

>Your daughter,
>Sylvia